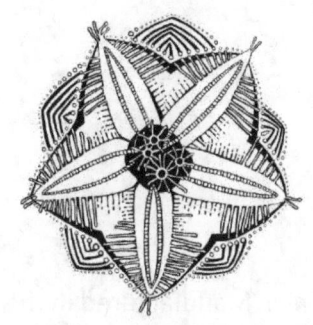

Hand Drawn

Adults Coloring Pages

Created By Ally Nathaniel

ISBN-13: 978-1517234744

ISBN-10: 1517234743

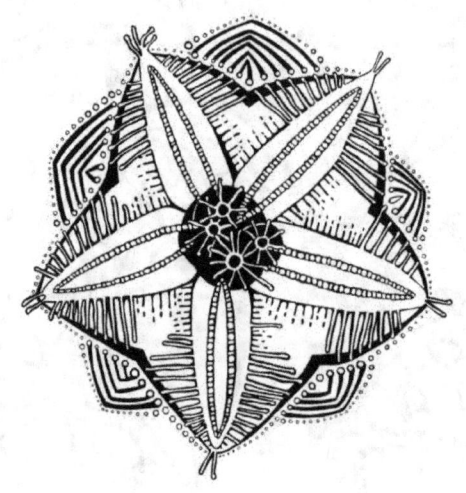

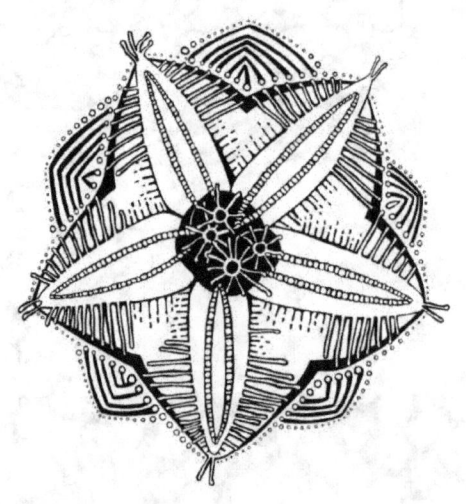

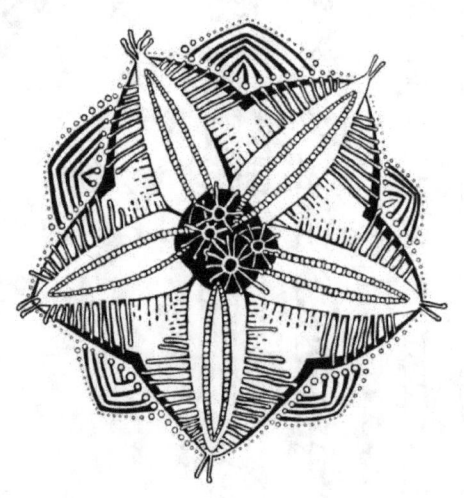

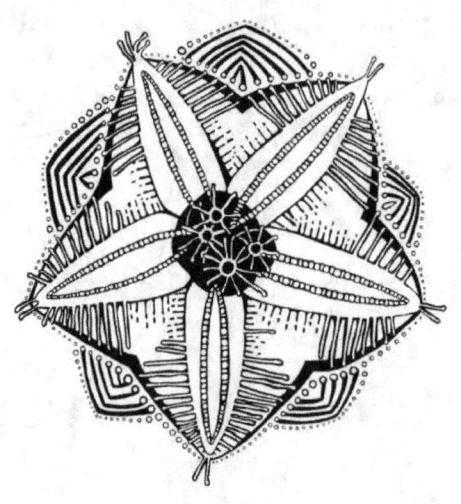

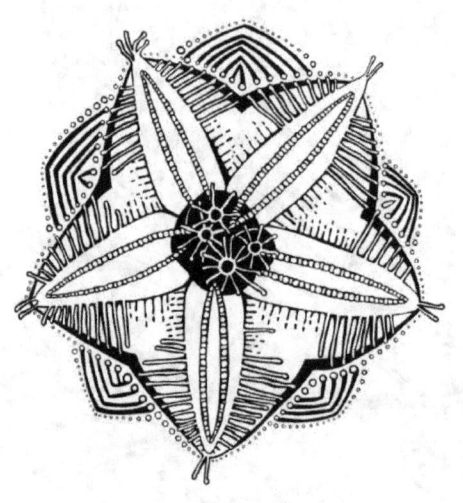

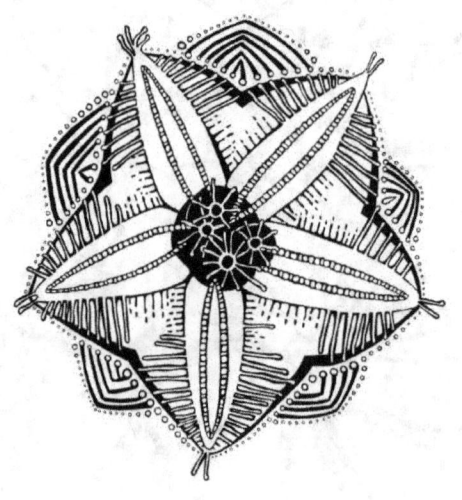

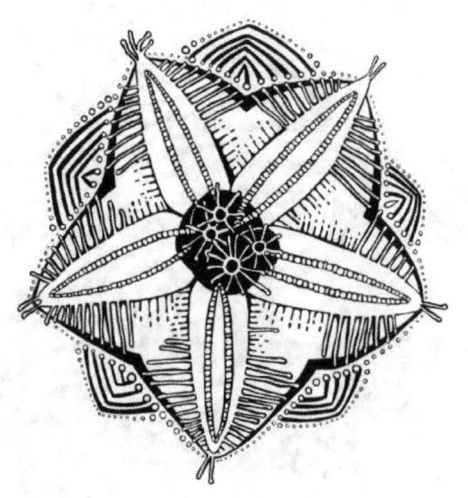

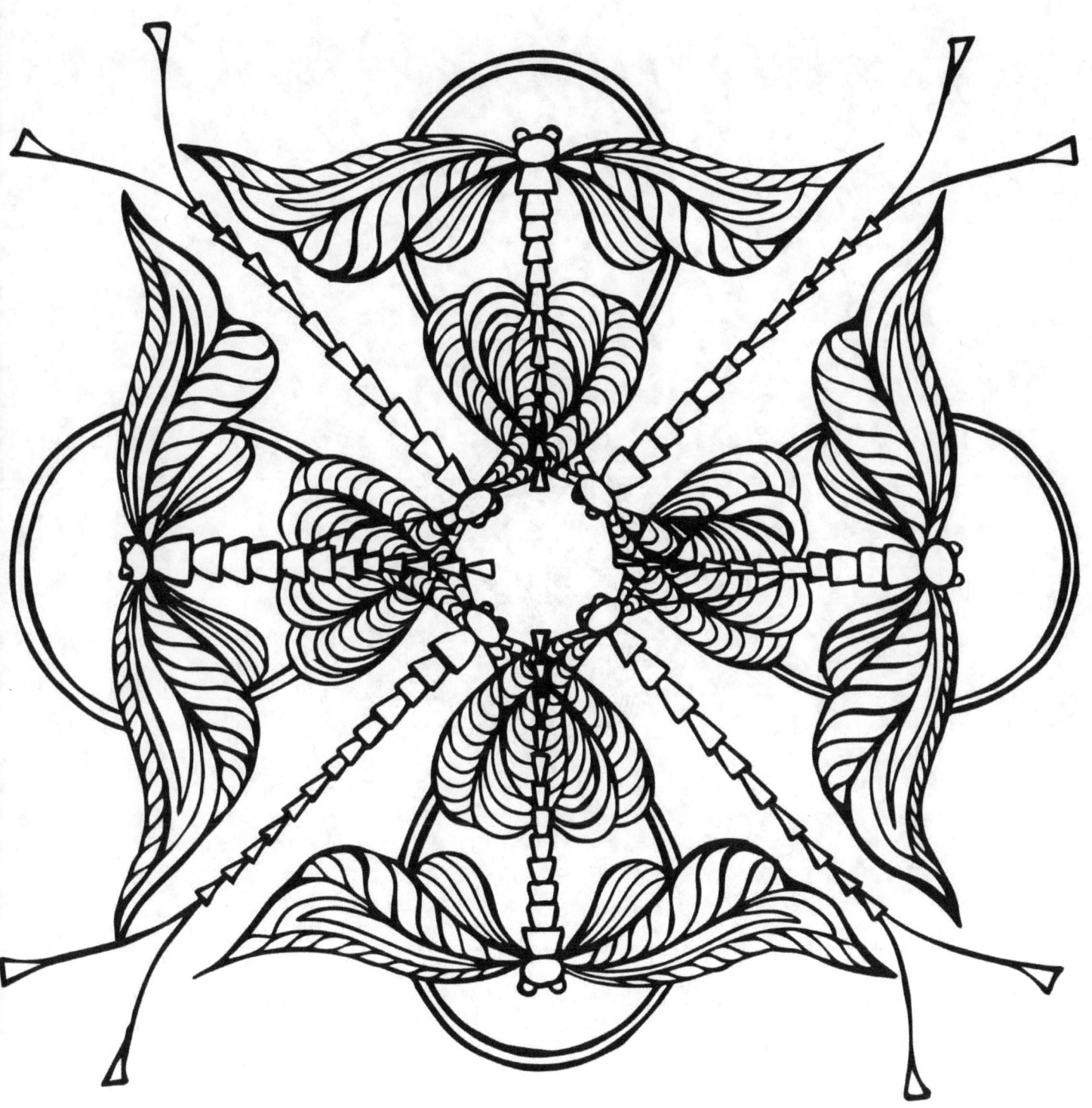

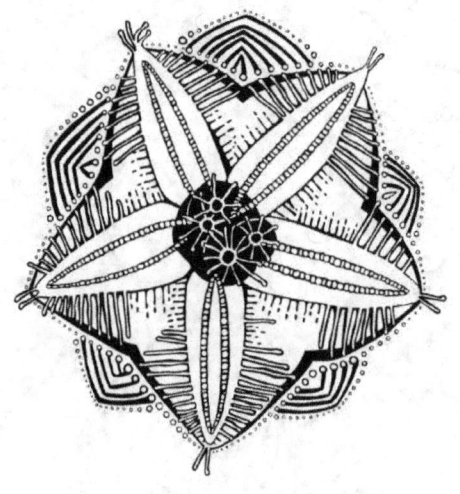

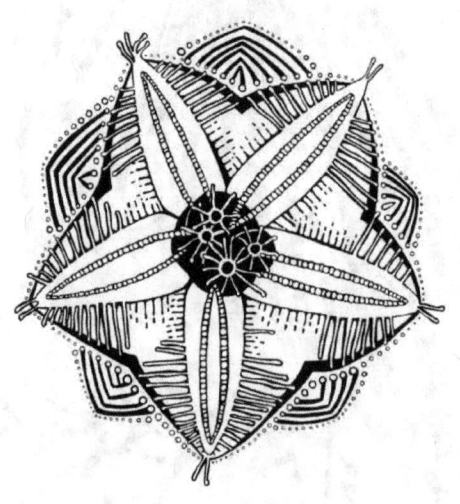

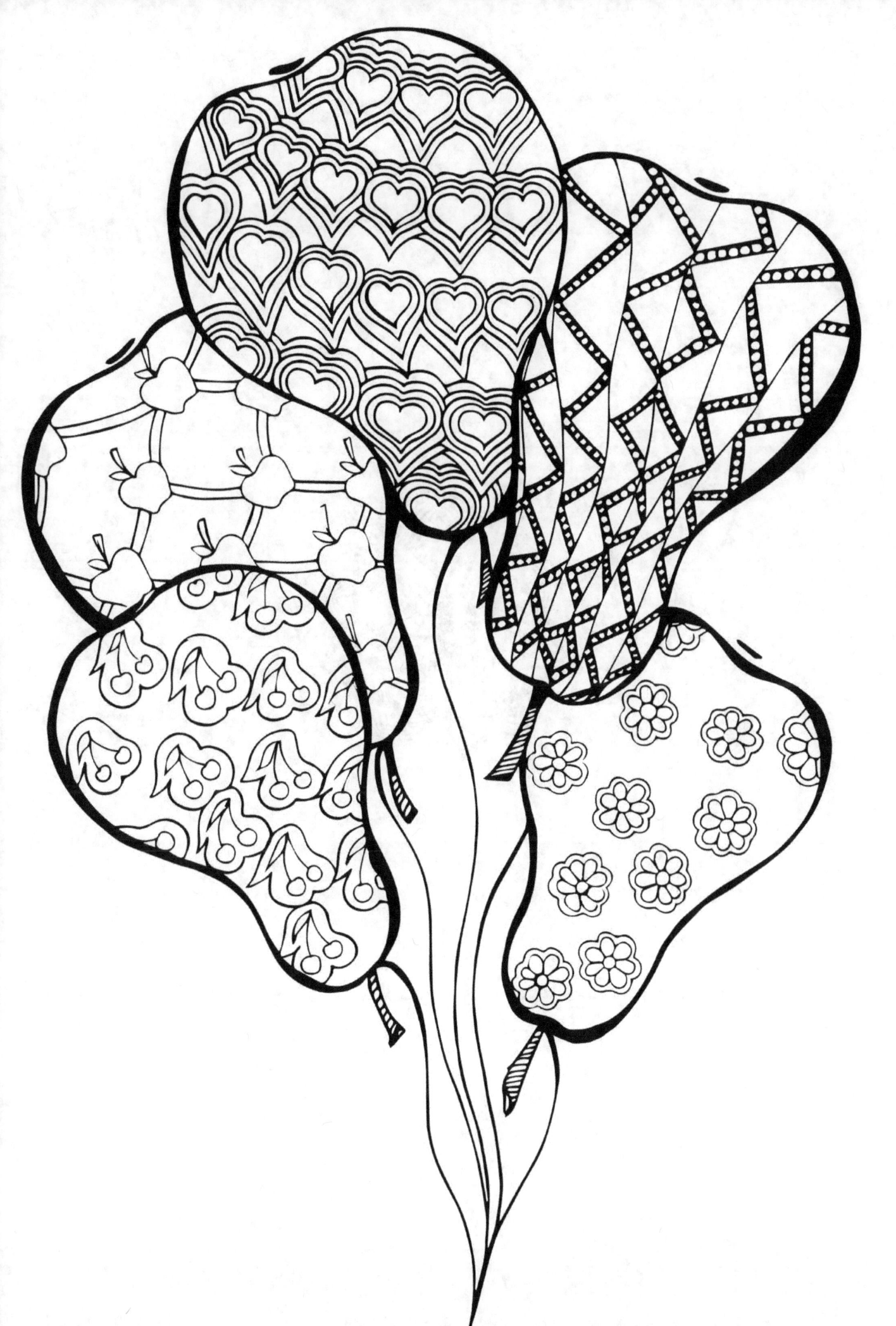

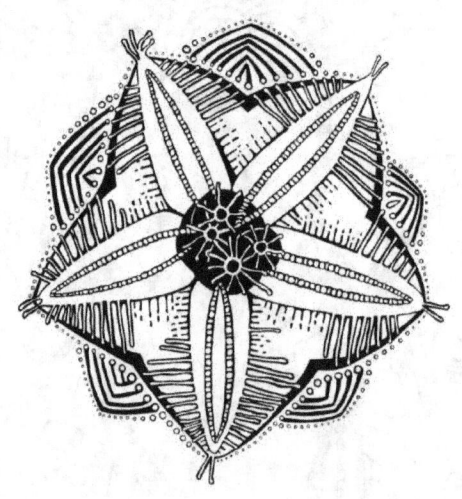

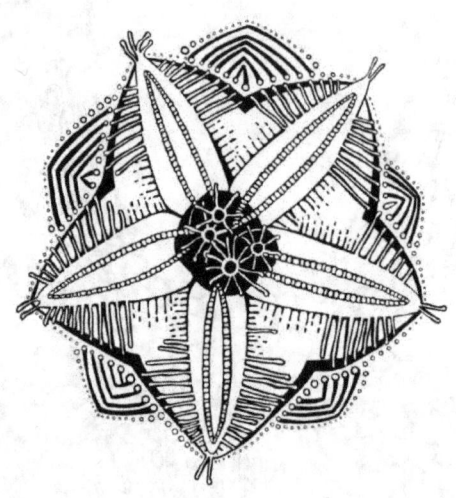

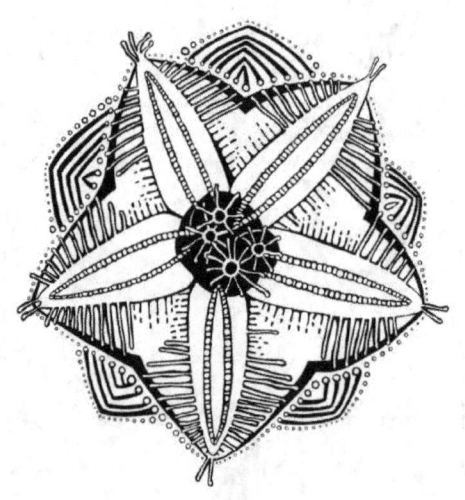

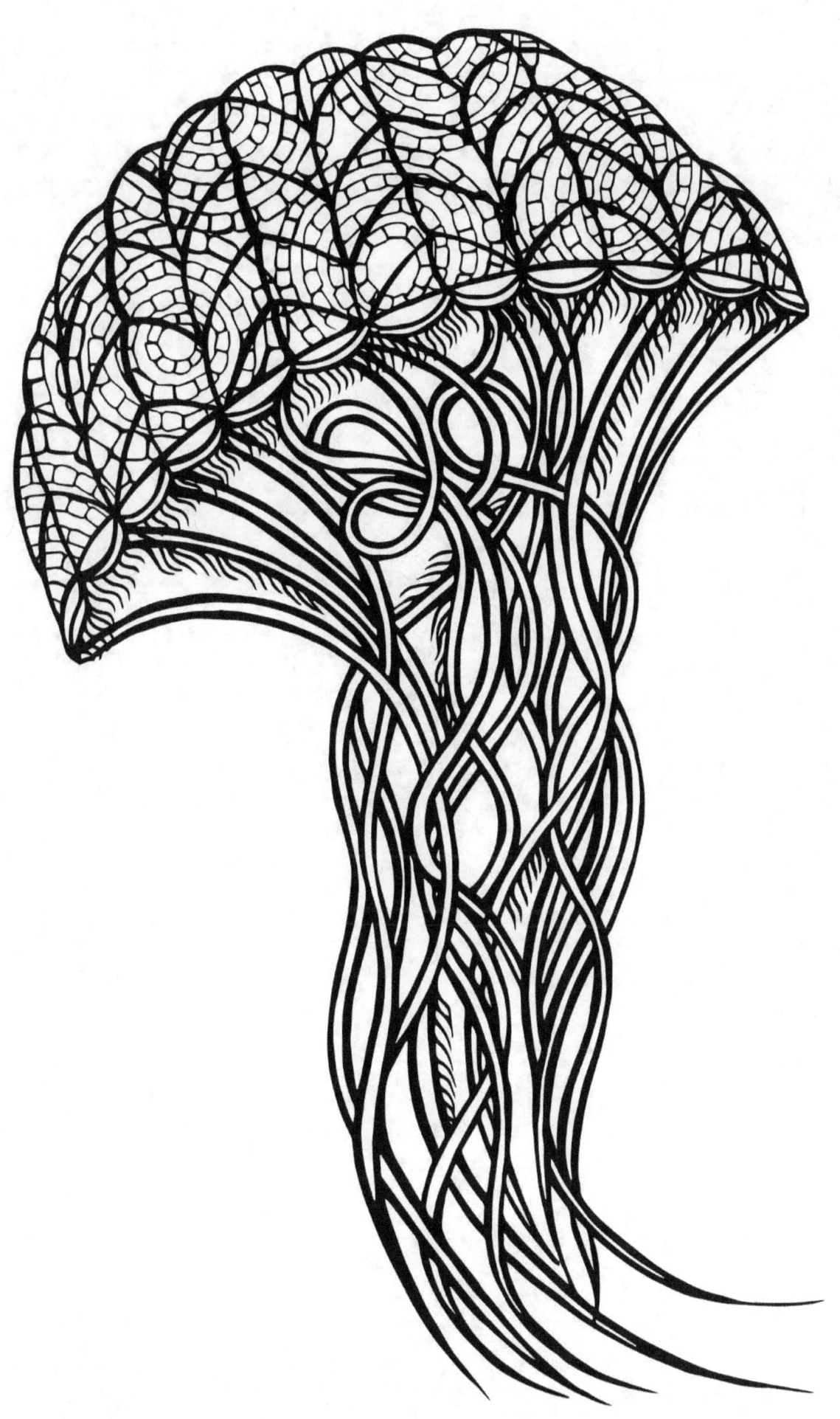

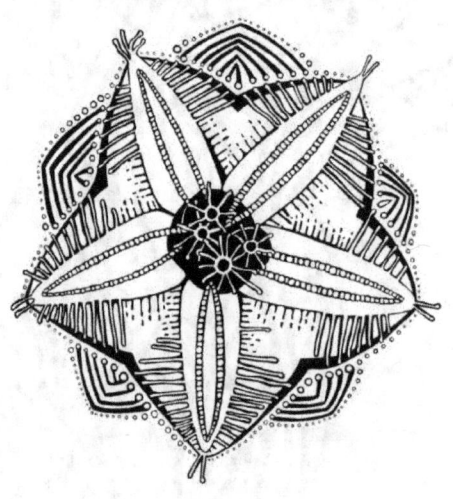

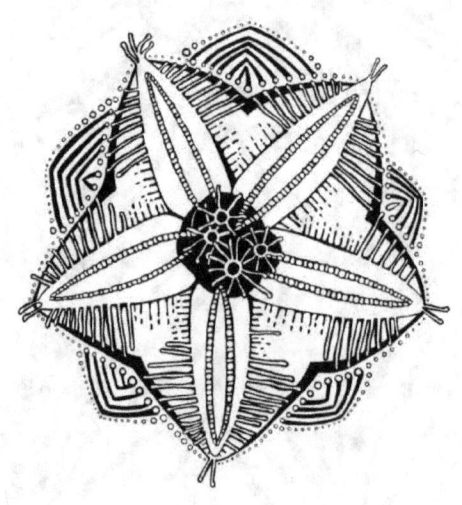

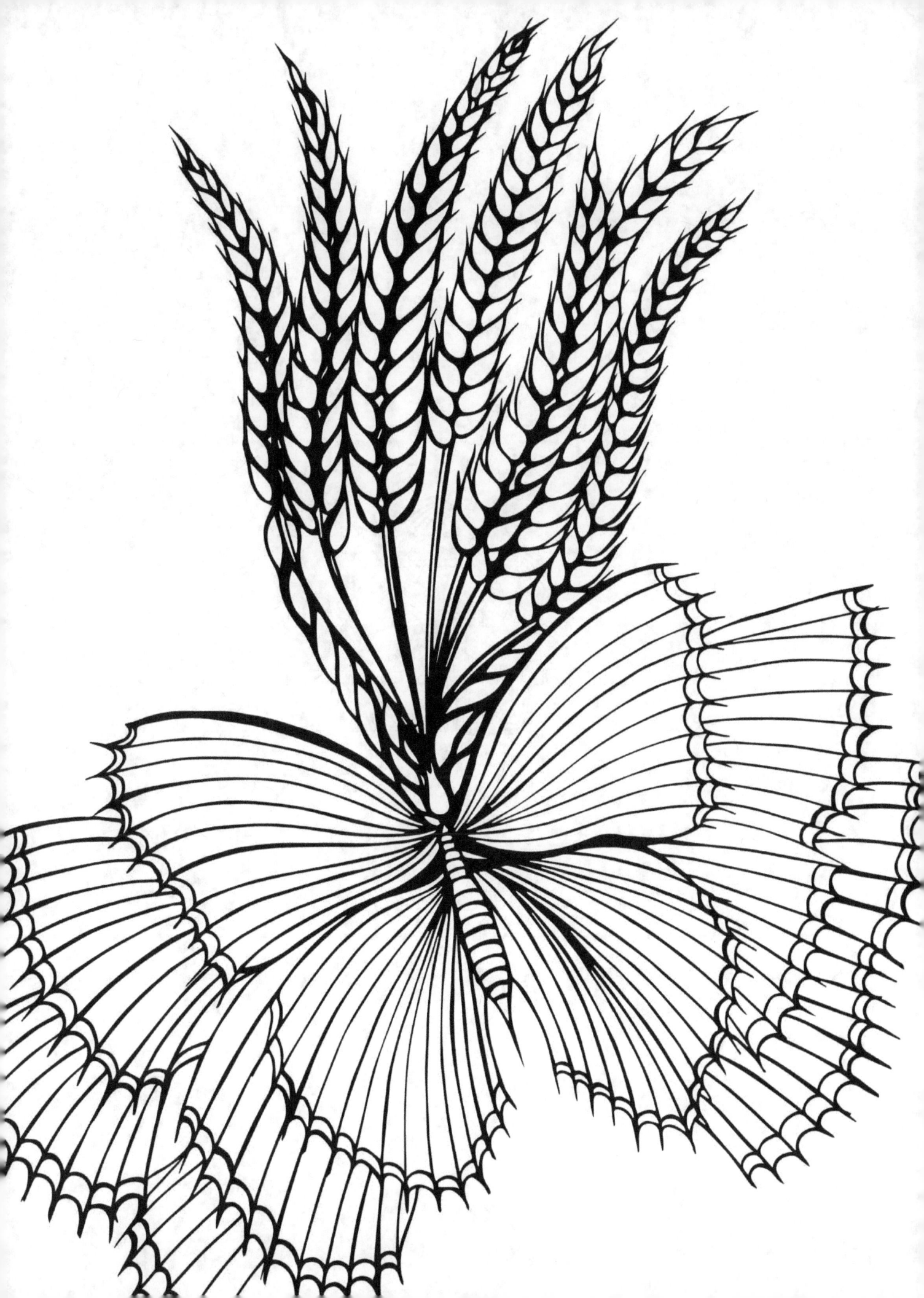

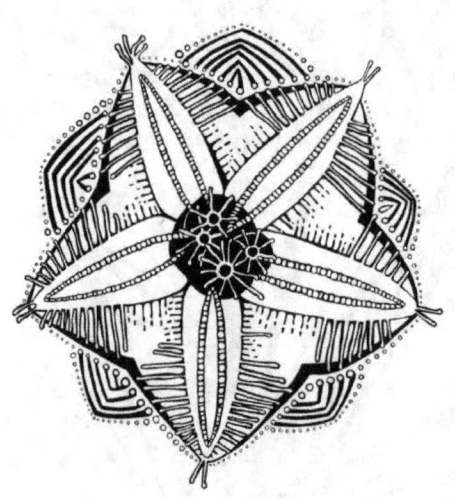

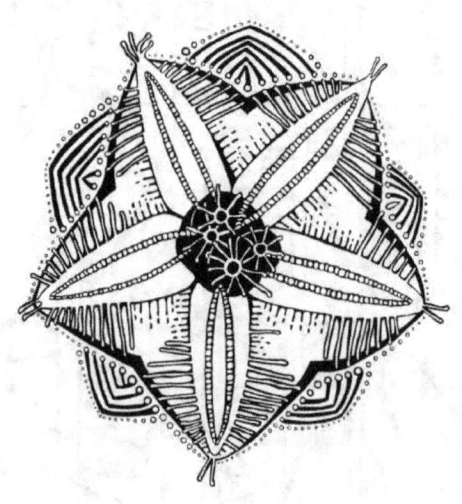

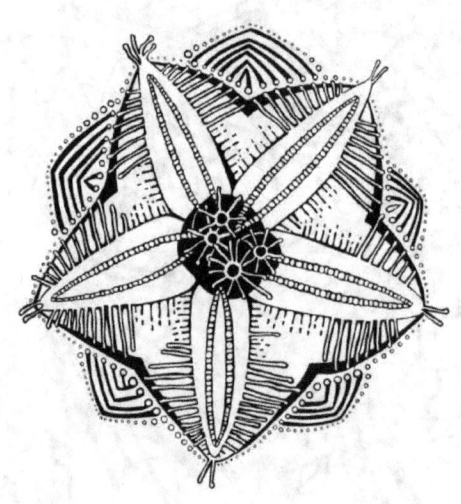

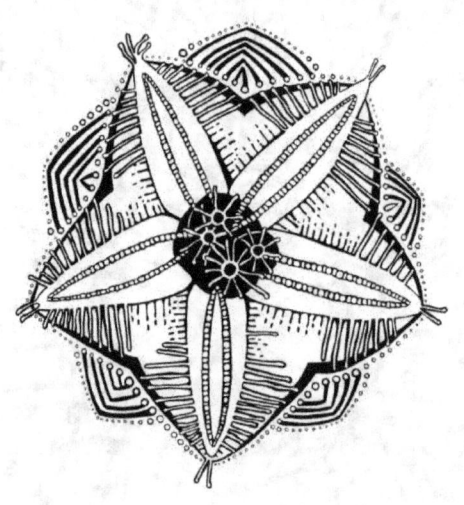

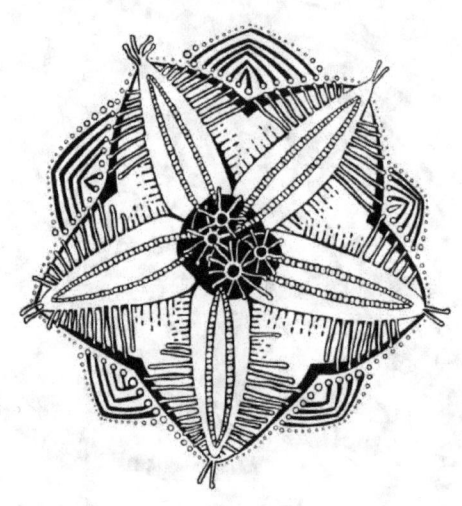

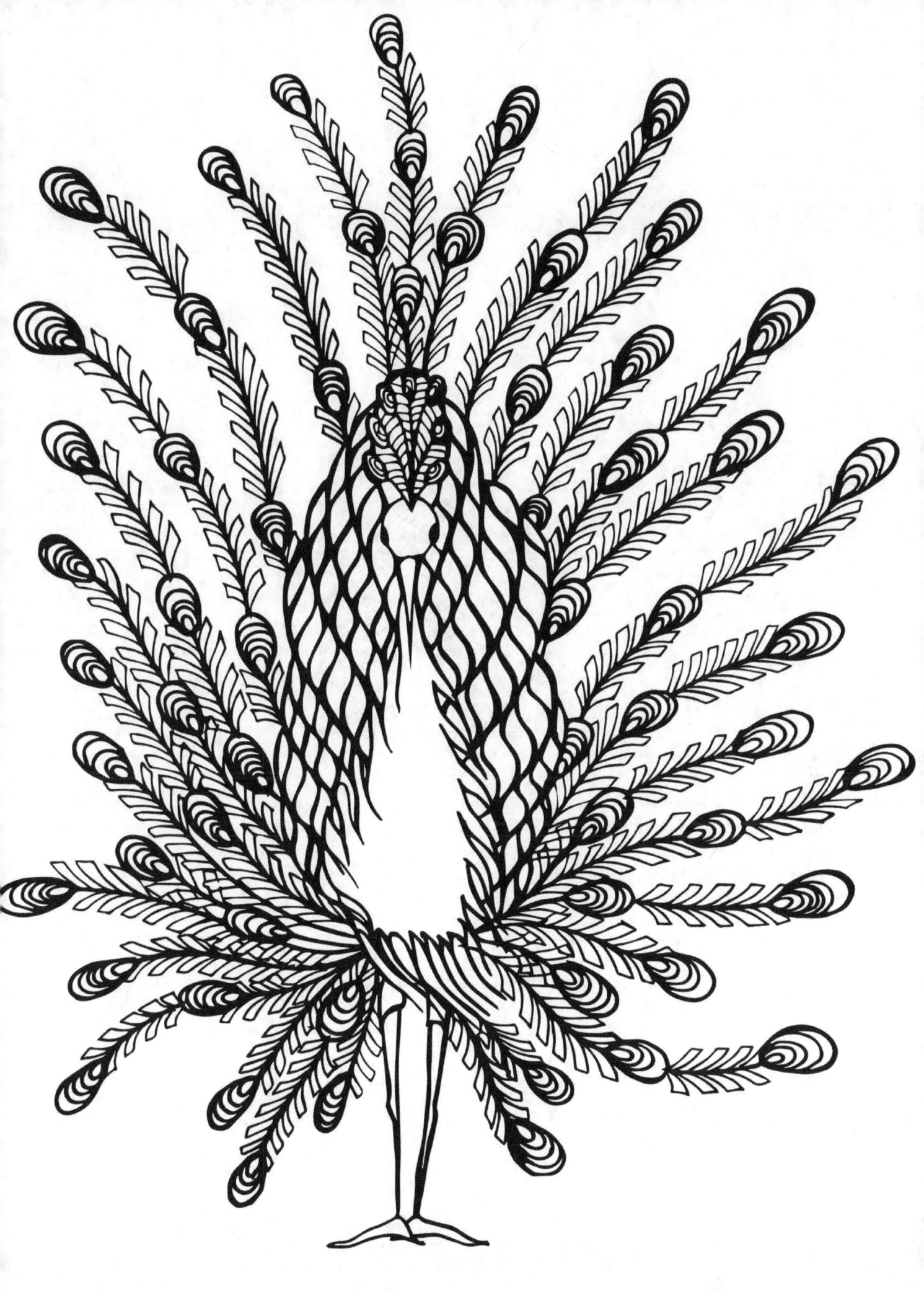

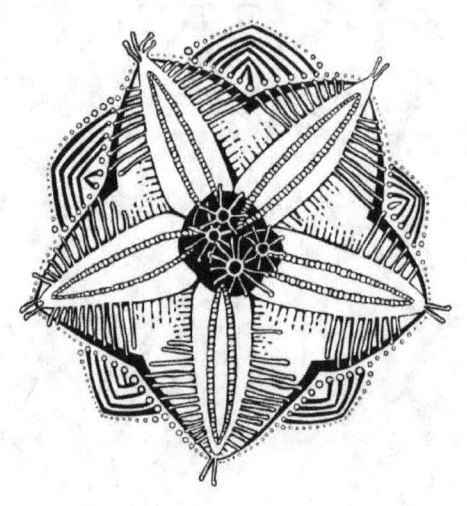

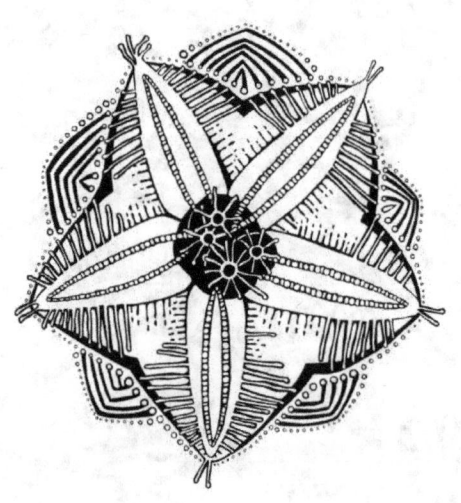

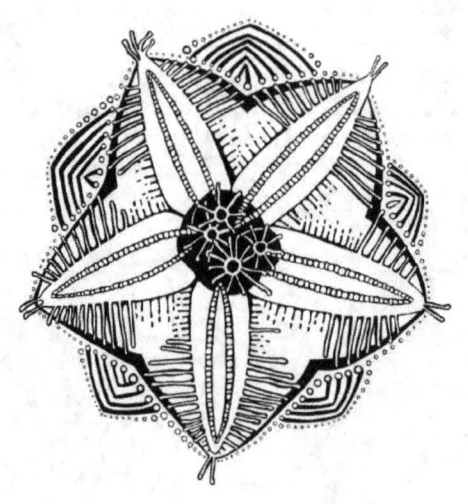

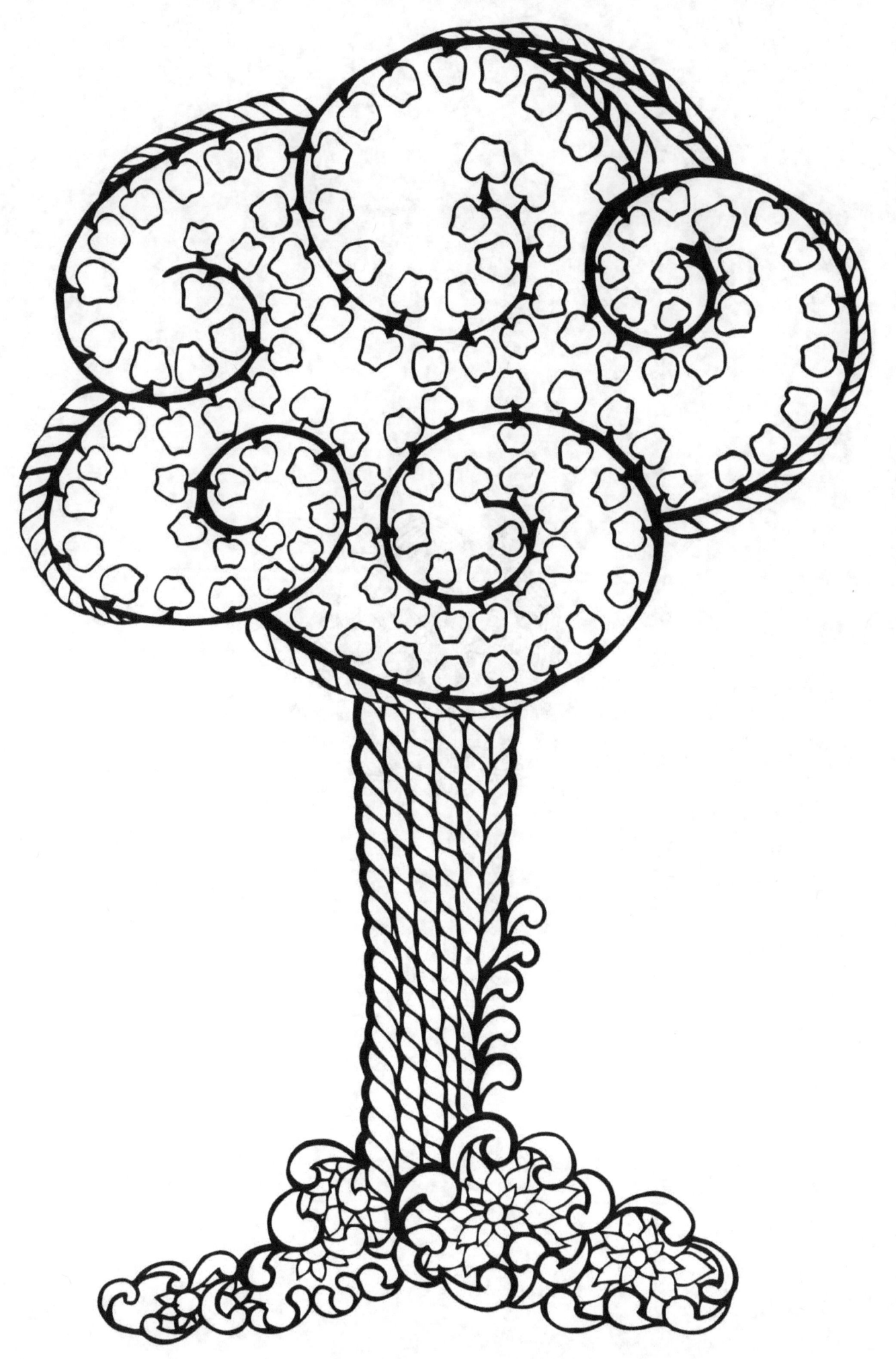

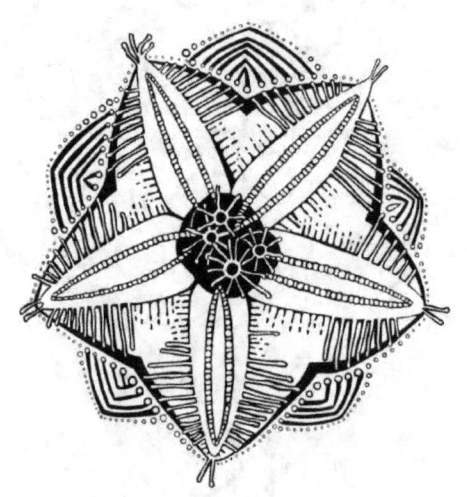

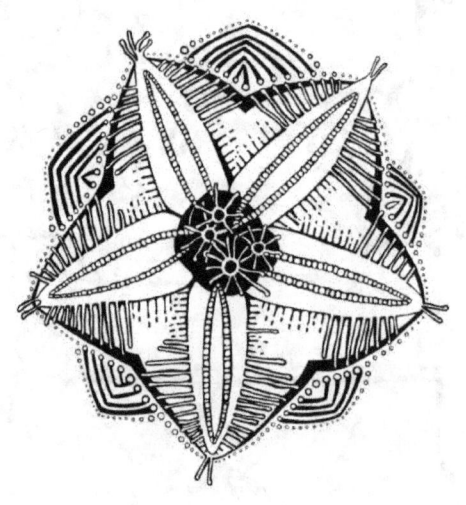

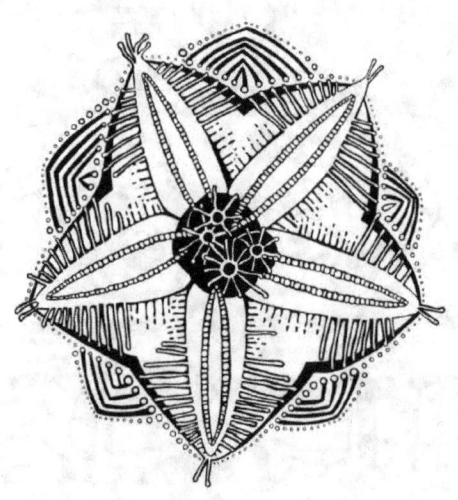

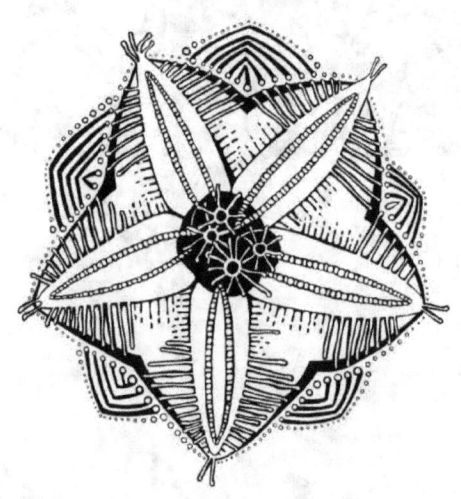

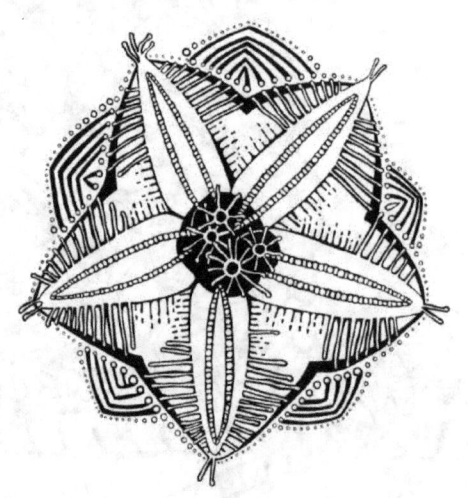

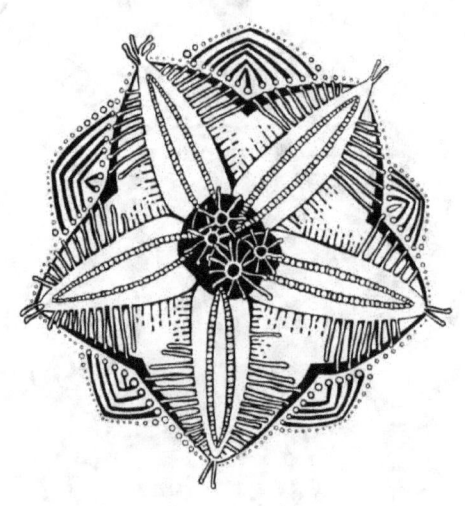

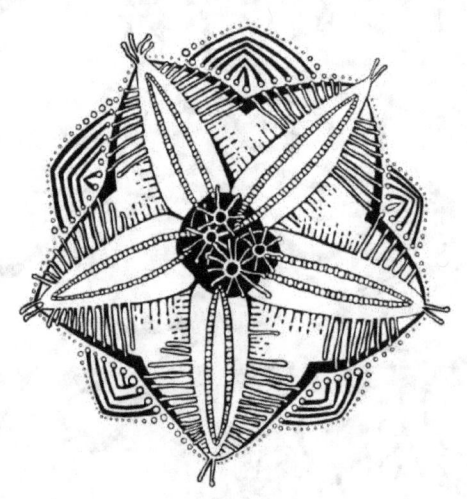

Thank you for purchasing this coloring book.
If you enjoyed it, please leave a review

on Amazon☺

Love,

Ally